Life's Pain
When God Is Silent
&
The
Power of
Prayer

Dr. David Scott

PURPLE CHAIR BOOKS
AND EDUCATIONAL PRODUCTS, LLC.

PCB

Published by Purple Chair Books and Educational Products, LLC
First Printing, 2020
Copyright © Dr. David Scott, 2020
Scott, David 1969-

Life's Pain
When God is Silent
&
The Power of
Prayer

By Dr. David Scott
ISBN 978-1-953671-00-4
Christian Life/ Motivational 1.Title

Printed in the United States of America
Set in Adobe Garamond Pro
Cover Designed by Kerry Watson
Interior Designed by Sarco Press

Publisher's Note

THE PURPOSE OF this publication is to offer hope, encouragement, and an alternative worldview to life's most challenging and difficult situations from the Christian perspective. This book is sold with the understanding that the publisher or author is not engaged in rendering psychological, therapeutic, or other professional services. If corrective, psychological counseling or additional expert help is required, the services of a competent professional person should be sought.

Without limiting the rights under copyright reserved above, no part of this publication may be reproduced, stored in or introduced into a retrieval system, or transmitted, in any form, or by any means (electronic, mechanical, photocopying, recording, or otherwise), without the prior written permission of both the copyright owner and the above publisher of this book.

Contents

Dedication vii
Acknowledgment ix
Introduction xi
Chapter One: Life 1
Chapter Two: Pain 11
Chapter Three: Why Pain? 15
Chapter Four: Grief and Loss 19
Chapter Five: Prayer: What Is It? 29
Chapter Six: Why Pray? 33
Chapter Seven: The Key to Prayer 39
Chapter Eight: Believers 45
Chapter Nine: Waiting 49
Chapter Ten: When God Is Silent 53
Chapter Eleven: God Can Be Trusted 57
Chapter Twelve: God Is Concerned 61
Final Thoughts 65

Dedication

I DEDICATE THIS book to the ever-present memory of my little brother Derek Lamont Crawford. I had so many plans, dreams, ideas, and aspirations for you. Much too soon were those dreams halted. I am anxious and awaiting that great day to see your beautiful face again. Thank you so much for our time together and also your love and gentle presence. Thank you for being a tremendous source of inspiration. I love and miss you. I will see you again.

Acknowledgment

I WOULD LIKE to extend a special thank you to all who have proven and showed your love for me. I appreciate you more than words can express. To my beautiful, unique, courageous, and gracious First Lady Mrs. Tamara DeRamus-Scott, you are a joy and treasure in my life. Thank you for your continued and unwavering support. Also, I would like to thank all of you that doubted this work would ever come to be. You played a tremendous role in pushing me forward. Nothing fuels success like naysayers, people doubting and not believing in your dreams. Last, I would like to extend a gracious and sincere thank you from the depths of my heart to one of the greatest, bravest, and most amazing women I have ever known, Ms. Pat Smith. You are an inspiration, role model, and mentor to thousands. Your legacy will live on in the achievements of those you have touched.

Introduction

OVER MANY YEARS of ministry and serving people from all walks of life, I realize that men and women, no matter their station, cannot escape the inevitability of pain. No matter who we are, our backgrounds, or where we are from, we all will face our share of challenges, heartaches, and sorrows. Pain is just a part of life and human experience. The human experience is a saga and journey of unexpected events, circumstances, and scenarios.

For anyone experiencing it, you are not alone; for most of us, pain can be trying. However, God has promised that there is no pain, heartache, or suffering too big that he will not help and deliver. Not only will God be with us, but he will bring us peace. God has promised not only to help but also to wipe our tears away. Proving his love consistently, we can trust that he is compassionate. The Father loves his children and has called us his own. There is nothing good that he will withhold from us. All good things come from him, and he desires that we have and experience them. We can have it all if we ask. Whatever we lack in our lives is available. We have not yet received it because we have never asked.

As a father that loves his children, he wants us to bring our fears, worries, and concerns to him freely and often. The method provided us to dialogue and commune with him openly and confidently without restraint is prayer. Through prayer, we can speak to him publicly, reaching him anytime, no matter what we have done. We can boldly come, bringing everything to Him in Prayer. He will listen and provide comfort to our deepest sorrows, hurts, and pains. He is always gracious to us. He will not only hear but answer in kindness.

When life deals us the most painful of experiences, God is there even when we cannot hear him. His love is limitless. No matter how tragic, crippling, and devastating, we are never abandoned. When we feel alone, God is there! The Psalmist clarified that there is no place that God does not fill. The bigness of his essence makes it impossible for him not to be present. His magnificence fills even the heavens.

God allows situations and scenarios in our lives that cause us to grow and direct us to him. He has given us a tool that cannot be limited or hindered. We have been prayer, a power that can tear down walls and bring us immediately into the presence of the great God. He has given us a seemly simple but perfect tool and weapon of immense power to not only reach him but change the outcome of any situation and circumstance if we would only use what he has made available. We can have the perceived impossible if we would only pray.

Life's Pain When God Is Silent

&

The Power of Prayer

CHAPTER ONE
Life

"The Lord keeps you from all harm and watches over your life. The Lord keeps watch over you as you come and go, both now and forever" (Psalm 121:7-8).

The human experience called life is a collection of minutes, hours, and days filled with a multitude of both unique and common experiences. Throughout life, there will be good days, bad days, ups, and downs. We will all experience our share of happiness, sadness, unforgettable laughter, and unimaginable pain. Though there are few guarantees, one certainty is that we will all have our share of pain. Reflecting on the human existence, the writer wrote in Job 14:1: "Mortals, born of woman, are of few days and full of troubles." Written thousands of years ago, the writer's declaration of truth has withstood the test of time.

In the twenty-first century, a period of technological advances, opportunities, possibilities, and abundance, never imagined so many are suffering, lost, and frightened. For many, the source of pain is their inability to find purpose. For others they cannot find satisfaction. For others still, the cause of pain is their inability to find true happiness. Humans have grappled a long time to find answers to these age-old questions: Why was I born? What is the meaning of life? What does it all mean? What is the purpose of it all?

Answers for many of life's questions continue to elude men and women, offering no solution. Many have reasonably concluded life's only guarantees are death and taxes. For many, answers to life's most challenging questions provide only a bleak expectation for tomorrow. As a result, for them, the solutions are obvious. Pursue and accumulate as much as possible. Strive to be the best. Possess as much as you can. Work hard for material achievements. Drive the most expensive cars. Wear the most coveted brands. Gain a luxurious home in the best and most exclusive neighborhood, and attend the best school. Marry for beauty if love is not an option, and be the most attractive, no matter the cost. The goal is to be the most envied. Always play hard, and never forget the Golden Rule. The one that finishes with the most toys prevails. Is that not what it is all about, winning?

For the majority, it is the continuous striving and fighting to succeed within this temporary system that is the root of significant sadness. Studies have proven that even among so-called overachievers, particularly entrepreneurs, Thirty percent of the population suffers from clinical depression. Adding the issues of anxiety and attention deficit hyperactivity disorder (ADHD), those numbers exceed 49 percent. With all the so-called right boxes checked, there is often still a lack of wholeness and satisfaction. Money and wealth will never bring complete happiness, hope, and authentic joy. Tangible things meant to fill the void consistently produce emptiness and disappointment. Many of histories noted geniuses proved this reality. In repeated scenarios, despite immense wealth, they could never satisfy the deep longing in the soul. The forty-fourth President of the United States of America, Barack Hussein Obama, once said, "Focusing your life solely on making a buck shows a poverty of ambition. It asks too little of yourself. And it will leave you unfulfilled."

At no other time in history have men and women had such excess and abundance. There has never been such access to food, clothing, entertainment, travel, career choices, and social interactions. However, also, there have never been so many gripped by a sense of desperation, pain, and hopelessness. Statistics confirm this reality. According to the Center for Disease Control (CDC), depression affects 20 to 25 percent of all Americans over the age of eighteen in any year. In extreme scenarios, depression leads many to believe there is no hope or prospect of the future. As a result, significant numbers of people surrender to the darkness, freeing themselves of the pain they believe they can no longer endure. Sadly, suicide takes the lives of over 44,965 Americans each year. There is a death by suicide in the United States every twelve minutes, making suicide the tenth leading cause of death for all ages. For those that choose this method of escape, the experience of life has become overwhelming and unbearable.

In challenging and stressful situations, suicide, for many, seems the only plausible option when all appears lost. In moments of desperation and periods of extreme mental anguish, far too often, this permanent solution seems the most reasonable answer to a temporary problem. For those that choose this as an option, life has spun beyond their idea or perception of personal control. The pain has become devastating and crushing. They cannot imagine a safe place to turn. No consideration of the future seems plausible. They just want out. They want out of fear, despair, and pain. They cannot consider the fact that nothing lasts forever. All things end—even the reality of their present circumstance.

The writer states in Job 14:1: "How frail is humanity! How short is life, and how full of trouble!" As the writer implies, we will all have our share of troubles. For us all, life can be riddled with problems, and filled with surprises beyond our control. Some circumstances will shake the foundation of our lives, bringing us to our knees—the place where we can find and meet God. Pain enters our lives in many forms. It might be the unexpected loss of long-time employment, surprising news from a most recent medical visit, or the sudden diagnosis of a parent or sibling's terminal illness, cancer! It might be the sudden death of a spouse. Maybe it is a dreaded phone call in the dark of night informing us of the tragic loss of a cherished son or daughter. It is at these moments when life has no meaning, makes no sense, and seemingly has no purpose. During these times, we feel most desperate and alone. But these scenarios are all familiar to the human experience. These experiences are part of this thing called life.

Everyday life events include a sudden change in our own or the health of a family member. It could be the termination or loss of a much-wanted pregnancy or unexpected changes in a financial situation. It might be the untimely death of a close friend, foreclosure on a home or business, or adjusting to new physical limitations. Have you ever been lied on, plotted against, betrayed, or had your character assassinated? It might be the coming to terms with aging and the unexpected loss of a cherished loved one. For a parent, there is no comparable pain to the loss of a child, followed only by the terminal illness of a parent, spouse, or the death of a sibling. Yet, these shared experiences are moments when we most want to make sense of it all. These are also the moments when we most want to curl up, wither, and fade away. During these times, we feel most hopeless and overwhelmed with hurt and pain. However, the pain has so much to teach us. The Reggae music legend Bob Marley once said, "You never know how strong you are until being strong is your only choice."

Pain is an inevitable aspect of the human experience. However, our suffering is not senseless or without purpose. There is much that we can learn from our hurting. If nothing else, suffering increases our connection to humanity. From pain, we come to understand that we are not alone. We discover that it does not isolate our experience. We all experience pain. From our sorrows, we gain a more significant and in-depth understanding of ourselves and others. Pain and hurt can lay us bare, open, and vulnerable. Suffering and pain allow us to present and offer our true selves to each other. It will enable us to gain wisdom and a deeper understanding of what matters and the insignificance of so many things. Through suffering, we learn the perspective to encourage and inspire others as they endure and journey through a similar scenario or set of circumstances. Pain has a way of teaching us we are far more durable than we once believed. It forces us to stretch beyond our preconceived limitations. It forces us to face our fears, look them in the eyes, and move past them. Pain teaches us we can do what we once believed impossible. We can be crushed and not destroyed. Problems have the potential to transport us from a dark and stagnant place to a sphere of higher purpose, significance, and effectiveness.

Sadness and pain are an unfortunate but inescapable aspect of our human experience. However, a lifetime of situations and the testimony of countless friends convinced me that this life has no sorrow that heaven cannot heal. There is no situation, circumstance, or heart-wrenching moment that the hope and joy of heaven cannot mend. The greatest tragedy and mistake of non-believers is their willful, challenging, and deliberate rejection of the only authentic hope and remedy for the pains of life. Ignorantly, in their defiance, they reject the promise and comfort of Psalm 34:18: "The Lord is close to the brokenhearted; he rescues those whose spirits are crushed."

Even though men and women will believe the most absurd claims like the earth is flat or the moon is made of cheese, or also that humans evolved from apes, they find it challenging to embrace the truth of the risen Christ. This reality can release them from their bondage, heal their brokenness, and alter the trajectory of their entire life. Yet, without having witnessed evolution happen or any evidence of a continued evolutionary cycle or process, people willingly and readily believe that humans evolved from apes, and then magically stopped evolving. I find this interesting. Another absurd claim that people have historically been ready to wage war to support is the genetic superiority of one group over another. However, it is proven that humans are over ninety-nine percent the same in every way. Genius, intelligence, and brilliance are not isolated and have always manifested across all so-called ethnic groups. Last, and perhaps most interesting, is the fact that some maintain a trust in so-called gods made with their own hands: statues that can be carried around in pockets, having eyes that cannot see, ears that cannot hear, and hands that cannot touch. These are images that can be smashed and broken. These are no gods at all. The great king of Israel David declared in Psalm135:15-18:

> "The idols of the nations are merely things of silver and gold, shaped by human hands.
> They have mouths but cannot speak, and eyes but cannot see.
> They have ears but cannot hear, and mouths but cannot breathe.
> And those who make idols are just like them, as are all who trust in them."

These same men and women adamantly refuse to believe in the Christ of history, the ever-living hope of the entire world. Ignorantly, they reject the balm that heals the sick soul.

Without Christ, the hard and unexpected experiences of life overwhelm and consume, leaving us broken, empty, and void of hope, wallowing in anguish and despair. Without Christ, there is no hope, peace, or joy. The tangible and temporary things of this world leave us wanting. Nothing in this life can satisfy, comfort, or mend broken hearts or pained, hurting, sick souls. Nothing is capable of what only Christ Jesus can do. This truth prompted the loving savior to say in Matthew 11:28, "Come to me, all of you who are weary and carry heavy burdens, and I will give you rest."

When life is dismal, dark, and bleak, no amount of money, cars, sex, designer bags, clothes, shoes, coats, or jewelry can bring comfort or peace. This is a job for the specialist, Christ Jesus, the Prince of Peace. He can and will do it. He never fails! For everyone courageous to believe, no matter the circumstance, no matter the situation, there is hope. Biblical scriptures tell us not only does Jesus care, but he lives to make intercession on our behalf. He prays for us. Many are the afflictions of the righteous. However, God has promised to deliver us through them all. Though many of life's situations are unpredictable and sometimes emotionally crippling, we are never alone. We who believe have a friend that stands with us, closer than a brother. We have a risen and living savior. We have Jesus, our faithful friend.

Without hope in Christ, Jesus, the struggles and pains of life become crippling. Life itself becomes empty and pointless. In an attempt to cope, many turn to drugs, alcohol, gambling, and illicit sex, trying to find temporary fulfillment and relief. With an increasing perception of insignificance in this world, the thought of a bright tomorrow seems improbable. Without Christ, the experiences of spousal separation, divorce, loss of a loved one, terminal illness, and cancer, loss of long-time employment, loss of financial savings, house foreclosure, or a combination of these events are more than enough to debilitate with indescribable pain. However, we must never lose hope. God is for us!

Divorce

Divorce can be devastating. Often, there are no winners. Everyone walks away hurt. The impact of divorce can be life-altering for both spouses and traumatizing for the children involved. Though often resilient, divorce significantly affects children. The literature on how divorce negatively impacts children is extensive. Research has concluded that separation diminishes every area of a child's life and affects that child or children into adulthood. Sometimes, the effects of marital discord and family disruption are visible twelve to twenty-two years later, manifesting in poor relationships. There is also an increased likelihood of adolescents dropping out of high school and needing some aspect of therapy or psychological help. It does not matter who is accused of being at fault; everyone gets hurt.

The Italian model and actress Monica Bellucci once said, "When people divorce, it's always a tragedy. At the same time, if people stay together, it can be even worst". Divorce is always hard. However, God specializes in the hard things. He can do what no other can. Like Perry Mason (fictional Los Angeles criminal defense lawyer), in the courtroom of life's most challenging cases, Christ Jesus never loses. He heals the broken and mends the breach. He is impartial, never choosing sides. The Eternal One is a righteous judge, compassionate, and full of love and mercy. About his resolve, the writer says in 1 Peter 5:6-7 "Humble yourselves under the mighty power of God, and at the right time, he will lift you in honor. Give all your worries and cares to God, for he cares about you."

ILLNESS

Like divorce, facing terminal illness or the potential loss of a loved one is also a crippling experience. There are no words to express the heart wrenching and emotionally staggering feeling that comes with watching a loved one suffer and slowly slip away, hour by hour, and day by day. Instinctively, we long to take our loved ones' place rather than witness their suffering. In these moments, we can hardly grasp the depths and magnitude of our pain. For these experiences, the words "heartache" and "pain" seem too small and insufficient to convey what our heart feels. To express it adequately, it seems there should be more robust, more significant, or more magnificent words. However, there is no circumstance that God's presence cannot change. Even when incomprehensible, God, in his power, knows what to do, and he never fails. He may not show himself when we believe we need him most, but he is always on time.

During times of our most enormous difficulties, the pain can produce an overwhelming sense of panic and anxiety. The alarm results from the thoughts and ideas of the unknown. There are so many questions, fears, worries, and concerns about what tomorrow will bring. What will life be like without him or her? How am I going to make it? What is going to happen to me? Why is this happening? Will I be able to go on? What will this mean for my life? Each reaction is common and reasonable. However, in the storms of our experiences, we must learn to pray. We must turn to God for guidance, strength, and comfort. In the darkness of life, we must learn to dialogue with the source of all comforts.

There is nothing more substantial or higher than God's desire to help us in our darkest hours and amidst the struggles in the deepest valleys. All we need to do is invite him into our situations through prayer. Without hesitation, he will come, if we call. Though he is ever-present, and though he never slumbers, he awaits our invitation. Although he is fully aware of all things past, present, and future, he will never force his way into our lives. He is always there, but like the perfect gentlemen, he waits for our invitation through prayer, inviting him to come. Here are the words of David in Psalm 86:1-7:

> "Hear me, Lord, and answer me, for I am poor and needy. Guard my life, for I am faithful to you; save your servant who trusts in you. You are my God; Have mercy on me, Lord, for I call to you all day long. Bring joy to your servant, Lord, for I put my trust in you. You, Lord, are forgiving and good, abounding in love to all who call to you. Hear my prayer, Lord; listen to my cry for mercy. When I am in distress, I call to you, because you answer me."

CHAPTER TWO

Pain

"He will wipe every tear from their eyes. There will be no more death' or mourning or crying or pain, for the old order of things has passed away" (Revelation 21:4).

Although life will present us with surprising moments of incredible and unforgettable joy, we will also experience periods of tremendous and unexpected pain. When that pain manifests and hits us, it will often leave us questioning, wondering what to do next, and how we can move forward from it. The astounding truth of this reality became sobering clear to the world in January 2020 when every news and media outlet confirmed the tragic helicopter crash and loss of basketball phenomenon and legend Kobe Bryant, his prodigy daughter Gianna, and seven others. Along with Mrs. Bryant, her remaining three daughters, and the family members of the other seven, the world mourned, sorrowed, questioned, and attempted to cope with unimaginable pain and grief as best they could.

The pain of this moment and the days that followed were challenging and life-altering for many. This unexpected and untimely loss is, for many, still unbelievable and surreal. However, those that hope in God have the comfort of stable and unchanging truth. No matter the pain or magnitude of the burden, God is there. We can lay the weight of our sorrow on him. He will carry it for us because he is the great burden-bearer. The writer admonishes us in 1 Peter 5, "Give all your worries and cares to God, for he cares about you."

Though pain is a harsh reality of this temporal experience we call life, there is no hurt or sorrow too great for the power of heaven. There is no grief or sadness that heaven cannot heal. No matter how devastated, the writer of Psalm 34:18 assures us: "The LORD is close to the brokenhearted; he rescues those whose spirits are crushed." God is our always present help in times of our most significant trouble. The angel Gabriel told Joseph to call the child "Jesus" (Yeshua), which translates "Deliverer," because that is who and what he is: a savior to his people. Christ is a savior to all who trust and call on him. He is always ready and able to save us from the pains and heartaches we face. He is consistently willing and available.

Unexpectedly, we experience and encounter life's hurts and sorrows. Without warning, we receive unexpected disappointments, letdowns, and inconceivable losses. In many of these moments, we find ourselves overwhelmed, feeling hopeless, and emotionally destroyed. We perceive joy, peace, and hope gone. We resolve; there can be no better tomorrow. The dark clouds hang too low for us to imagine that the sun will ever shine again. It is during these times that God's love, compassion, and power are most available. During these moments, the words of Jesus ring loudest in Matthew 11:28 "Come to me, all of you who are weary and carry heavy burdens, and I will give you rest."

No matter the situation or scenario, all pain and heartaches have a purpose. If we believe that God is good, we must know that he is right. Not sometimes, but at all times. Familiar with misery and loss, the great Viktor Frankl once said, "If there is meaning in life at all, then there must be meaning in suffering." He said, "Forces beyond your control can take away everything you possess except one thing, your freedom to choose how you will respond to the situation." We can believe that God is always with us and has a brilliant plan and purpose for all of our experiences. We never have to lose hope, and give in to the weight and trial of the moment.

Amid our most significant trials, we can believe that God is still with us and that he cares for us. It is our choice to find that the great and loving Father is in control of everything and that whatever he has permitted us to experience has meaning, purpose, and value in our lives, even when we cannot imagine or conceive it. Despite the inescapable pain in our lives, God is still good. David reminds us of God's goodness in Psalm 103:7-16, saying:

> "He revealed his character to Moses and his deeds to the people of Israel. The LORD is compassionate and merciful, slow to get angry, and filled with unfailing love. He will not constantly accuse us, nor remain angry forever. He does not punish us for all our sins; he does not deal harshly with us, as we deserve. His unfailing love toward those who fear him is as great as the height of the heavens above the earth. He has removed our sins as far from us as the east is from the west. The LORD is like a father to his children, tender and compassionate to those who fear him. For he knows how weak we are; he remembers we are only dust."

CHAPTER THREE
Why Pain?

"BECAUSE WE ARE UNITED WITH CHRIST, WE HAVE RECEIVED AN INHERITANCE FROM GOD, FOR HE CHOSE US IN ADVANCE, AND HE MAKES EVERYTHING WORK OUT ACCORDING TO HIS PLAN" (EPHESIANS 1:11).

PEOPLE OFTEN BLAME God when they experience pain. Mistakenly, when people experience challenges, they believe it punishment. However, this is not the case. Sadly, this is a concept and idea most of us learned from our parents, people we valued and trusted, and others we allowed to influence our understanding of the divine. Though many of them were well-intentioned, they were grossly misinformed about the actual character and nature of the God of the Bible (Yahweh/YHWH). God is loving, compassionate, and kind. His very essence is love. Because he loves so perfectly, he does not cause pain, even if he permits it. Whatever God allows, there is a purpose. God does not make mistakes, nor is he surprised. The Eternal One is omniscient. Before the world took shape or form, he was aware of each of our unique experiences. Everything, including pain, has a purpose in the divine plans of God. The Lebanese American writer Khalil Gibran once said, "Out of suffering have emerged the strongest souls; the most massive characters are seared with scars."

Pain has a way of becoming one of our most significant teachers. From the challenges of life, we learn transformative lessons. Without pain, we would never gain a needed perspective. Hurt and suffering have the power to teach us the most about ourselves. Through pain, we come face to face with our most authentic selves. Our suffering humbles, strips, and lays us bare. Through trials, we reveal unknown strengths, limitations, and weaknesses. Mother Teresa once said, "Pain and suffering have come into your life, but remember the pain, sorrow, and suffering is but the kiss of Jesus, a sign that you have come so close to Him He can kiss you." Pain is rarely the end. Often it is merely the beginning of a new experience that God has divinely orchestrated.

There is always a purpose for the challenges we face. After the trial has ended, it will produce in us what God intended. It will achieve his intended aim, making us better. Nothing we encounter is by chance. He knows and is attentive to even the minutest details. Scripture reminds us that God is the beginning and end of all things. He declares in Revelation 1:8 "I am the Alpha and the Omega—the beginning and the end," says the Lord God. "I am the one who is, who always was, and who is still to come—the Almighty One." God is aware of all things, and always there.

God never uses pain and temporary suffering to destroy us, but he uses it to bring us to our knees. Strangely, only when we are humbled can we accept the obvious. We need God. In those moments, God's use of pain is most significant. Without discomfort, we might never commune with God. Without pain, we might never come to depend on God nor experience the magnitude of his power. We might never invite him into our lives. Pain forces us toward God. Through trials and struggles, we learn to seek him. Through suffering, we gain the privilege of knowing him as a deliverer, healer, comforter, provider, Lord, personal savior, and friend. Pain teaches us the benefit of cultivating an intimate and personal relationship with the eternal God and his Christ. God longs for fellowship, whispering to us often. However, he screams through pain and calamity, getting our attention.

Many lessons we learn through the experience of pain we could learn no other way. The Swiss-American psychiatrist Elisabeth Kubler Ross once said, "The most beautiful people we have known are those who have known defeat, known suffering, known loss, and have found their way out of those depths." Knowing each of us intimately, God orchestrates events and circumstances that bring us to the place he desires. He uses the difficulties of our lives to form and shape our spiritual growth and development. When we allow it, pain brings us to maturity and a place of reliance on him.

CHAPTER FOUR
Grief and Loss

"HE HEALS THE BROKENHEARTED AND BANDAGES THEIR WOUNDS" (PSALM 147:3).

W<small>E USUALLY ASSOCIATE</small> grief with life's most meaningful and significant losses. Though an inevitable circumstance, a loss is never comfortable. When we lose something cherished, logically, we experience and bear the pain of the thing lost and no longer part of our routine or a regular part of our lives. This is particularly true when we experience one of the most significant sources of grief, the loss of a loved one. When we lose a loved one, we are never entirely the same. Life's dynamics and paradigms are changed forever.

In some strange way, there seems something almost cruel about using the word "loss," particularly when mentioning our dear and beloved. When something or someone is separated or snatched from us, there is no right way to explain what or how we feel. We do not have or possess appropriate or sufficient vocabulary to convey the emotions. At that moment, we think they left us behind to cope with their memories, their scent, their things, the indelible marks and traces they leave in our hearts, and the immeasurable emptiness in our lives. There is a myriad of feelings, emotions, and mental scenarios that we encounter because of this traumatic reality. For each of us, the experience of loss is different. No two encounters are the same. However, the similarity we share is the indescribable sense of grief.

When we experience the devastation and trauma of loss, we transition through various stages. We consider these stages of emotions an internal defense. They are our innate coping mechanism, as we attempt to adjust, manage, and come to terms with the reality of our present situation. Even when the scene makes little sense, and we struggle to come to terms with our existence, we can take comfort because God has a plan and a commitment to bring us again to a place of peace and happiness. Pain and grieving do not last forever. We read in Psalm 30:5 "Weeping may endure for a night, but joy comes again in the morning."

In efforts to cope with loss, we eventually move through what we call the seven distinct stages of the grieving process: shock and denial, bargaining, guilt, anger, depression, acceptance, and hope. Commonly, most people will identify with some, if not all, of the seven, identified stages as they grieve. Though there is no particular order in which any of us grieve, initially, all of us are naturally *shocked* and in disbelief, finding the gravity of the situation complicated to grasp when first presented with surprising news, particularly of death. When life presents us with tragic scenarios, understandably, we struggle to find meaning.

If the grieving process adhered to any order, the second stage of that process is *denial.* Personal loss is always challenging and stressful. Because of the difficulty associated with grief, it is not uncommon for this stage of the grieving process to last varying lengths of time. We all move at our own pace. For some, this stage can be long and for others brief. It is crucial to understand and recognize that each step of the grief process will take different lengths and lasting periods. Conceivably, there might be times when the duration of the first, second, and third stages lasts just a few moments, while others last much longer.

The third stage of *bargaining* is something many of us do. It is not uncommon for us to negotiate the change or alteration of a situation that is the source of our grief and pain. Bargaining has its roots in the thought process, "What could I do to reverse the loss?" or "Take me instead." We move to a position of wanting to avoid the pain by extreme or illogical measures. Though the desired outcome is both improbable and impossible in most cases, it is natural and universal to respond in such a manner.

The fourth stage of the grieving process is *guilt,* which often presents itself in a manner closely associated with the previous stage of bargaining. During the phase of guilt, we often irrationally blame ourselves for unexpected circumstances. Although we can recognize that the event is outside our control, we still struggle with feelings surrounding guilt for either being in this situation or scenario, being unable to avoid it, or having no control over it.

When the fifth stage, a*nger,* presents, it is assumed and reasonably expected that a person is progressing and steadily coming to terms with specific realities. Previously, none of the other stages have been external. They have all been inward responses. By contrast, anger is considered more of an outward expression. Anger is understandably a familiar and relatable emotion, often masking the weight of inexplicable sadness and pain.

When grief and pain are associated with loss, during the grieving process, there can be a reasonable expectation of varying degrees of *depression*, which is the sixth stage. In contrast to the previous definitions, depression traditionally is not classified as a stage. There is no particular time or duration for depression. Depression can come and go throughout the whole grieving process. However, what is most interesting about depression is that usually when the stage of anger subsides or has passed, depression will also dissipate.

After all, the previous stages have been worked through, marking the seventh stage of grief, finally *acceptance, and hope* return. When acceptance and hope return, this signifies the point in the process in our pain that we recognize and accept the fact that our reality has changed permanently: that life will never be the same. We come to terms with the fact that we now have a new normal. We accept and embrace the fact that there will be a need for specific changes, adaptation, and adjustments. However, we can perceive hope and the possibility of a brighter and more meaningful future.

We are presumed to move and to make a successful transition through each of the seven stages. However, this is not always the result. It is not uncommon that sometimes we get stuck unable to move. It is also not uncommon to step back and forth between the stages, lingering for long periods. When the pain and grief are too deep and overwhelming, we often cannot move in any direction without God. During those times, it is God alone who aids and helps us. Without faith and hope in God, when tragedy grips us, we can find ourselves on a sea of sorrow, aimlessly adrift like ships without sails.

With God, all things are possible. When paralyzed by pain and fear, God holds the answer. He provides the balm for our deepest pain if we come to him in prayer. He alone can bear our burden and extend comfort when we chose to be consoled. We have this assurance in Psalm 37:5 "Commit everything you do to the Lord. Trust in him, and he will help you." We can tell him about our struggles, hurts, and pains. He never sleeps and never slumbers. He is anxiously waiting to ease our pain. The writer admonishes us in 1Peter 5:7, "Give your worries and cares to God because he cares about you." Those that believe in him have an open invitation to bring every burden, hurt, and sorrow to him. God has repeatedly proven that nothing is too hard for him if we would only bring it to him in prayer.

A Personal Request

If I may, I would like to share with you my testimony of the power of prayer and how God can mend a broken heart, extend comfort and peace, and give a believer hope amid life's toughest storms. I am a witness that God can do anything for us if we would only pray. He has no respect for the person. He shows no favoritism. All can come to him, just as we are. We are all invited and welcomed to come boldly to his throne of inconceivable grace.

My Testimony

While driving home late one night, I received a phone call that would change my life forever. I answered the phone. The voice on the other end was labored, pausing between every other word. I struggled to not only under the words but identify the voice of the caller. It was my brother-in-law, but my sister's screams distracted me in the background. Her cries in the distance made my heart flutter. I could feel my body getting warm all over. Each pause on the phone felt like an eternity. My sister's distress was warranted. My baby brother had been shot and killed earlier that morning while sitting at a traffic light on his way to church. Many years later, I can still feel the poignant sting of disbelief that washed over me at that moment. Even now, it feels as if it were yesterday.

Unlike the relationship many rival siblings share, I loved my little brother immensely. Because of the fourteen-year age difference between us, he was more like a son to me. I was there at the hospital on the night he was born. I remember vividly the moment he made his grand and speedy entrance into this world. We arrived at the hospital. Soon, my mother was escorted away by nurses. Derek was born less than an hour later. He was always moving fast in that way. Form the day he was old enough to leave the house, I would wrap him in a blanket, get his diaper bag, and take him with me almost wherever I went, long before he was a toddler or able a walk. Because of our closeness, I guess it should be no surprise that I was the first to see him enter this world, and the last one to see him on the day he departed.

On that morning, we ate our last breakfast together and had our final brother-to-brother chat. I remember that my little brother was tired that morning, but he went along anyway. Perhaps he just wanted to make me happy. Maybe he knew that was his last breakfast and heart to heart talk with his big brother. On that morning, I remember that there was something in his eyes, something in his laughter and tone. It was a seriousness I had not seen before, a kind of melancholy. I guess he knew he would not be staying here much longer. I think that shared breakfast, despite his tiredness, was his way of saying, "I love you." And, "I won't be seeing you again for a little while." When the phone rang, my mother was riding with me in the car. Intuitively, before I could say a word, she knew what the caller had said on the other end of the phone. Trying to hold myself together, still in disbelief, I turned to her and took a deep breath. I remember her words. She calmly asked, "Is it, Derek? Is he dead?" My response: "Yes, ma'am."

I watched her tenderly fold her face in her hands, merely saying, "Oh my God." I felt helpless and desperate. I immediately got off the freeway and began to pray. I realized there would be challenging moments, hours, days, months, and maybe even years ahead. However, in that moment of uncertainty and sadness, I needed God to take control. As I called out to him, sitting in that car on the side of the road, instantly, the power, strength, and presence of God enveloped both my mother and me, giving us indescribable peace. As never before, we both experienced a peace that surpasses all human comprehension. We both shared the peace that Jesus spoke of in John 14:27 when he said, "My peace do I give to you, not as the world gives." In that moment of prayer, his love was a balm to our wounded hearts. When we needed him most, God proved he was not only a mender of broken hearts but that he also could be reached and touched at any moment in prayer. I know fully understand David's declaration in Psalm 118:5 "In my distress, I prayed to the LORD, and the LORD answered me and set me free."

For my brother, Derek Lamont Crawford, we did not have a funeral. We had a triumphant memorial service. We rejoiced and celebrated the life loaned to us for twenty-two years, and we reveled in the tremendous power of God that we experienced through the power of prayer. I am a living witness that prayer can and will make a difference in any situation. There is no circumstance or sorrow so deep that God cannot reach and heal. God's power is both matchless and immeasurable. When asked, "Is there anything too hard for God? Can God do it? The answer comes from a host of witnesses in response, "There is nothing too hard for God. Yes, God can do it!"

In life, there are many kinds of losses. The most common include the loss of a close friend, death of a partner, death of a classmate or colleague, terminal injury or illness of a loved one, divorce or breakup, death of a family member, abruptly leaving home or community, debilitating injury or illness, loss of health, death of a pet, loss of a job or career, sudden relocation, moving away from friends after graduation or marriage, or losing resources and financial security and stability. Any of these or any combination can be a source of significant and overwhelming grief and sorrow.

Today, as never, there is the constant threat of company downsizing, layoffs, and termination of employment. These realities cause astronomical anxiety, pain and fear. No one should experience the trauma caused by losing a primary source of income. However, it is a daily reality and experience for many. Gone are the days of job security, regardless of loyalty, dedication, and deliberate preparation and sacrifice. Gone are the days of the assured pension, 401k, and the gold watch at retirement. Everything in society has changed.

Death and taxes are the only certainties that remain, and the sure promises of God. Man can offer not certainties or guarantees no matter how deliberate his intentions. History has informed and assured us that even the best laid plans of men go astray. God alone is faithful. His word is always true and reliable. Whatever he says, he will do. His word is immutable. The writer says in Isaiah 40:8:"The grass withers, the flower fades, but the word of our God will stand forever." What he has promised he will perform. He will be with us. Nothing can separate us from his love. He loves his children. We can be confident that we have security in God. He holds the future. He will never abandon us or his word, nor will he ever fail.

As a culture, we have embraced the fallacy that people are best defined by what we possess or what we do professionally. At introductions, people rather ask about the person. They primarily are interested in what the person does. It is all too common to hear someone ask, "So what do you do?" Sadly, we attribute worth and value by education, career, vocation, and economic status. As a result, we strive to develop, cultivate, and excel to the highest pinnacles, never realizing or considering the devastating impact of these things abruptly taken away. Losing these insignificant things is the source of pain and grief for so many. For most, the sadness is overwhelming. Many have been so seduced by the trappings, materialism, and consumerism of this world that the idea of doing without the latest, greatest, and so-called best is inconceivable. Countless people have placed their hope in the wrong things, forgetting the words of the prophet recorded in Job 1:21: "I came naked from my mother's womb, and I will be naked when I leave. The Lord gave me what I had, and the Lord has taken it away. Praise the name of the Lord!"

Despite our failures to recognize God's goodness toward us, He remains gracious and kind. No matter the circumstance, God is always there, willing to comfort us in our times of trial and adversity. Despite our shortcomings, it is his will that we prosper. The writer says in Psalm 35:27: "Let them continually say, "Great is the Lord, who delights in blessing his servant with peace!"Nothing brings greater joy to the Father than his children's glad and joyous hearts. It is for that reason we are told to come to Him. All things separate from him ultimately disappoint, falling significantly beneath his best for us. However, in his presence, we will consistently find the completeness of joy.

God does not cause grief. However, he allows situations to arise, offering us the opportunity to experience him intimately. He facilitates scenarios, leading us to dialogue with him through prayer. Prayer is not a monologue. We make our petitions, and he answers. Prayer is the mode of communication given that allows us to share our hearts, passions, and pains. Prayer shows our willing submission and acknowledges a need for God's guidance, direction, and strength. Our willingness to pray acknowledges our understanding that he is higher, more significant, and more prominent than us. Through prayer, we demonstrate and acknowledge our need and dependence on our Father.

God does not delight in the pain of his children. However, he uses suffering to bring us into his presence. He uses everyday situations to force us to our knees, allowing him the opportunity to reveal his perfect and divine plans. Without cause, rarely do we turn to God. We fancy ourselves as sufficient little demigods, in need of nothing outside ourselves. He then reminds us it is he who has made us. We are not our own designers. Despite ourselves, in fellowship with him, he leads us to peace, hope, and comfort. The writer said in Psalm 16:11: "You will show me the way of life, granting me the joy of your presence and the pleasures of living with you forever." Through the petition of prayer, we call him. In response, he, who is always faithful, never fails. He will always answer!

CHAPTER FIVE
Prayer: What Is It?

"When you pray, go away by yourself, shut the door behind you, and pray to your Father in private. Then your Father, who sees everything, will reward you" (Matthew 6:6).

Prayer is communication. It is a dialogue between God and us. Prayer is not merely a monologue in which we are the only ones speaking. Prayer is a conversation. We talk, and God responds in the way he chooses. He speaks audibly, and other times he speaks through his word, and to our hearts. He is the master communicator. He said to the prophet Elijah in 1Kings 19:11-12:

> "Go out and stand before me on the mountain." And as Elijah stood there, the Lord passed by, and a mighty windstorm hit the mountain. It was such a terrible blast that the rocks were torn loose, but the Lord was not in the wind. After the hurricane, there was an earthquake, but the Lord was not in the earthquake. And after the earthquake, there was a fire, but the Lord was not in the fire. And after the fire, there was the sound of a gentle whisper."

God will always answer. Sometimes it is just a small, gentle whisper. He is always speaking to us, his beloveds. We only need to be still and listen to his voice.

Though sometimes God seems to remain silent, he can still speak. Even when we think God is silent, He is still talking. In his silence, he is teaching a lesson of patience or merely saying, "Wait." When he is ready, he will respond to our request, petitions, and pleas. He is never late. He is the perfect Timekeeper, always appearing on time, because his time is still the ideal time. He spoke to Moses from behind a burning bush. He spoke to the apostle Paul from a blinding light while he traveled along a Damascus road. He spoke from the heavens saying, "This is my beloved Son, in whom I am well pleased."Undeniably, he can talk. When God chooses silence (or so it seems), it does not mean that he is not there or that he is unconcerned. It is merely a delay for the moment he had predetermined before the world began. He would never leave us nor forsake us. God's answer will come; it is only sometimes delayed. The writer says in Daniel 10:12-13 that after the angel appeared, he said these were to the prophet:

> "Don't be afraid, Daniel. Since the first day you began to pray for understanding and to humble yourself before your GOD, your request has been heard in heaven. I have come in answer to your prayer. But for twenty-one days, the spirit prince of the kingdom of Persia blocked my way. Then Michael, one of the archangels, came to help me, and I left him there with the spirit prince of the kingdom of Persia."
> We must always remember that when we pray in faith and belief, God hears and immediately responds. Even if the solution is immediate, wait, or not now, he will answer.

Prayer is how we make our request known to the eternal God. Only through prayer, are we able to tell God the concerns of our hearts and minds. By this method, we acknowledge we need God and depend on his divine wisdom. In our humility and submission, we imply that we have come to the end of ourselves and need his help. Through this act, we admit our limitations and declare our trust and hope in him. Through prayer, we affirm confidence in the declaration he made to his people in Jeremiah 29:11: "I know the plans I have for you, declares the Lord, plans to prosper you and not to harm you, plans to give you hope and a future." (NIV) Through prayer, we concede to God's authority and welcome his response in the way he chooses, accepting that he knows what is best for us.

Prayer is the greatest weapon in an arsenal for coping with the pressures and circumstances of this uncertain, challenging, and often pain-filled life. Prayer is the source of our peace during the most demanding conditions, no matter how difficult or seemingly hopeless. Prayer has the power to bring peace in the most blistering of life's storms. There is nothing higher than the power of prayer. French surgeon and biologist Alex Carrel (1873-1944) once said: "Prayer is a force as real as terrestrial gravity. As a physician, I have seen men lifted out of sickness by the power of prayer. It is the only power in the world that overcomes the laws of nature."

God is always faithful. If we call Him in prayer, he will answer. The Eternal One is attentive to the cries of his people: those who hope and believe in him. The writer says in Psalm 145:18-19: "The Lord is near to all who call on him, to all who call on him in truth. He fulfills the desires of those who fear him; he hears their cry and saves them." Through prayer, we reach the presence and throne of God. By petition, we invite him into our lives, circumstances, and situations. He gladly receives our invitation. As a loving father, he promises never to cast aside those who come seeking him in prayer. The writer says in Hebrew 11:6: "It is impossible to please God without faith. Anyone who wants to come to him must believe that God exists and that he rewards those who sincerely seek him."

No matter how seemingly insignificant our prayers and petitions, God listens. He is always waiting, eager to hear from his children. Nothing will negate the irrefutable fact that he is a loving father, full of compassion and grace. Jesus says in Matthew 7:9-11: "You parents-if your children ask for a loaf of bread, do you give them a stone instead? Or if they ask for a fish, do you give them a snake? Or course not! So if you sinful people know how to give good gifts to your children, how much more will your heavenly Father give good gifts to those who ask him." He affirmed his love in Matthew 21:22, saying, "All things you ask in prayer, believing, you will receive." It is God's great pleasure to meet the needs of his beloved children. As a loving father, He longs to see us glad in Him.

CHAPTER SIX
Why Pray?

"IN MY DISTRESS, I PRAYED TO THE LORD, AND THE LORD ANSWERED ME AND SET ME FREE. THE LORD IS FOR ME, SO I WILL HAVE NO FEAR. WHAT CAN MERE PEOPLE DO TO ME? YES, THE LORD IS FOR ME; HE WILL HELP ME" (PSALM 118:5-7).

WHEN WE PRAY, we ask God to help and deliver, fight for us, intervene for us, and move on our behalf. Through prayer, we dialogue with the sovereign creator of the universe. With prayer, we tell God, "I need your awesome power. I am reaching and stretching toward the one that is higher and greater than I." The very act of prayer is an act of humility and submission. Prayer offers us the privilege of tapping into the power and possibilities of the universe. In the worship of prayer, we whisper into the ear of the divine. Jesus, the Lord's Christ, the Word of God made flesh, showed us the power and necessity of prayer. Being (God the Son), wrapped in the tissue and humanity of a man while on earth, having authority and control over all things, still prayed to God the Father in heaven.

The scriptures present several examples of Jesus' dependence on prayer. The writer says in Matthew 26:36, "Jesus went with them to a place called Gethsemane. He told the disciples, "Sit down here while I go over there and pray." The writer says in Mark 1:35: "In the early morning, while it was still dark, Jesus got up, left the house, and went away to a secluded place, and was praying there." Speaking about those that opposed and wanted to harm him, Luke 6:11-12 says: "But they were filled with rage and discussed together what they might do to Jesus. It was at this time that He went off to the mountain to pray, and He spent the entire night in prayer to God." Before he died and returned to heaven, recorded in John 17:1-5:

> "Jesus spoke these things; and lifting His eyes to heaven, He said, "Father, the hour has come; glorify Your Son, that the Son may glorify You, even as You gave Him authority over all flesh, that to all whom You have given Him, He may give eternal life."This is eternal life that they may know You, the only true God, and Jesus Christ whom You have sent." I glorified You on the earth, having accomplished the work which You have given Me to do."Now, Father, glorify Me together with Yourself, with the glory which I had with You before the world was."

Jesus spent immeasurable time in prayer. How much more should we? There is nothing too big or too small to bring to God in prayer. Prayer invites God, relinquishing our control, removing the limitations of our freedom. When we pray, we welcome God to take complete control of our messes, even at our hesitation. We should never forget God is always attentive to the prayers of the righteous. The Lord promises in 2 Chronicles 7:13-14:

> "If I shut up heaven that there be no rain, or I command the locusts to devour the land, or if I send pestilence among my people: If my people, which are called by my name, shall *humble themselves, and pray*, and seek my face, and turn from

their wicked ways; then I will hear from heaven and will forgive their sin, and will heal their land."

God has chosen prayer because it is a weapon that cannot be stopped or hindered when coupled with faith. The writer says in 2 Corinthians 10:4: "The weapons we fight with are not the weapons of the world. On the contrary, they have divine power to demolish strongholds." There is no situation or circumstance that prayer cannot change. The scriptures provide us with many examples of the power of prayer in the lives of individuals not much different from you or me.

In 1Samuel, the writer tells us of a woman named Hannah, who suffered the pain and heartache of not being able to bear children. Through the power of prayer, Hannah changed her destiny. The scripture says in 1 Samuel 1:9-12, 19-20:

> "Once when they had finished eating and drinking in Shiloh, Hannah stood up. Now Eli, the priest, was sitting on a chair by the doorpost of the LORD's temple. In bitterness of soul, Hannah wept much and prayed to the LORD. And she made a vow, saying, "O LORD ALMIGHTY, if you will only look upon your servant's misery and remember me, and not forget your servant but give her a son, then I will give him to the LORD for all the days of his life. Early the next morning, they arose and worshiped before the LORD and then went back to their home at Ramah. Elkanah lay with Hannah, his wife, *and the Lord remembered her*. So with time, Hannah conceived and gave birth to a son. She named him Samuel, saying, "Because I asked the LORD for him."

Prayer is not only important; it is essential. The Bible tells us in Luke 18:1: "Men ought to always pray, and not faint." Men and women should routinely and regularly spend time in prayer. Speaking to the necessity of prayer 1Thessalonians 5:17 tells us to "pray without ceasing." This passage implies the cultivation of a praying spirit. One defined by the adoption and development of a standard posture of spiritual humility before God, continuously crying out to our Father for help, direction, and preservation. Through prayer, we trade the limitations of our abilities for the inexhaustible power of the sovereign God. With prayer, Joshua changed history. The writer says in Joshua 10:12-14:

> "On the day the LORD gave the Amorites over to Israel, Joshua said to the LORD in the presence of Israel: "O sun, stand still over Gibeon, O moon, over the Valley of Aijalon. So the sun stood still, and the moon stopped, till the nation avenged itself on its enemies, as it is written in the Book of Jashar. The sun stopped in the middle of the sky and delayed going down about a full day. There has never been a day like it before or since, a day when the LORD listened to a man. Indeed the LORD was fighting for Israel!"

The scriptures admonish us to pray in every situation. We could make no better decision than to consult the creator of the universe, the keeper of time past, present, and future. Humans are weak, often arrogant, and ignorant of their frailties. But prayer is immeasurably powerful. For that reason, the Holy Spirit prays for us, making intercession to God the Father on our behalf. The scripture tells us in Romans 8:26: "The Holy Spirit helps us in our weakness. Often we do not know what to pray for in most situations. But the Holy Spirit prays for us with groaning that cannot be expressed in words."

WHAT WE GAIN FROM PRAYER

There are many benefits, and so much we gain from prayer. Through prayer, we develop a deeper relationship with God. Prayer also helps us gain a greater understanding of God's plan, will, and purpose for our circumstances. Through prayer, we learn to embrace and accept God's will, even when it is difficult. Prayer helps us gain insight into the character and loving nature of God. Through prayer, we get the often necessary strength to hold on and not succumb to the temptation and sin of doubt. Prayer helps us gain the right perspective, allowing us to receive God's promise of a measure of extended grace, peace, and a comforted mind. Prayer helps us find answers and direction. Prayer welcomes the matchless power of the Holy Spirit into our lives and helps align our will with Gods, making us more like Christ Jesus, who said, "Not my will, but you're will be done."

Prayer stretches us, causing us to grow in many unexpected ways. Prayer helps us improve by deepening our fellowship with God. Prayer helps us grow in expectation and confidence that God will supply all of our needs. The apostle Paul declared in Philippians 4:19: "This same God who takes care of me will supply all your needs from his glorious riches, which have been given to us in Christ Jesus." Prayer helps us grow in understanding and experience of God's grace, compassion, and favor. Prayer also helps us grow in spiritual wisdom, the ability to have internal joy despite our situation, and strength.

Through prayer, we touch the heart and majesty of God with our petitions. When we humble ourselves and pray, he will hear from heaven and heal us. The Lord is impartial. When we pray and have faith, he always listens. We make prayer most effective by faith. The writer says in Hebrews 11:3 and 6:

> "By faith, we understand that the entire universe was formed at GOD's command and that what we now see did not come from anything that can be seen. And it is impossible to please GOD without faith. Anyone who wants to come to him *must believe that God exists* and that he rewards those who sincerely seek him."

For those that trust, believe, and hope in him, nothing is impossible. To those that have faith, Jesus says in Luke 11:9-10:

> "I tell you, keep on asking (in prayer), and you will receive what you ask. Keep on seeking (in prayer), and you will find. Keep on knocking (in prayer), and the door will be opened to you. For everyone who asks, receives. Everyone who seeks finds, and to everyone who knocks (prays), the door will be opened."

CHAPTER SEVEN
The Key to Prayer

"DON'T WORRY ABOUT ANYTHING; INSTEAD, PRAY ABOUT EVERYTHING. TELL GOD WHAT YOU NEED AND THANK HIM FOR ALL HE HAS DONE. THEN YOU WILL EXPERIENCE GOD'S PEACE, WHICH EXCEEDS ANYTHING WE CAN UNDERSTAND. HIS PEACE WILL GUARD YOUR HEARTS AND MINDS AS YOU LIVE IN CHRIST JESUS" (PHILIPPIANS 4:6-7).

THE PRACTICE OF prayer is a spiritual tool and a weapon of immense power. However, it is most effective when the essential keys to its activation are incorporated. Though it is God's limitless power that works on our behalf, prayer requires our participation. To activate God's power in our petitions, we must ask with a sincere heart, be confident that God can, and have authentic faith. Without faith, which is the key, our prayers are often ineffective. The writer says in James 1:5-7:

> "When you ask him, be sure that your faith is in GOD alone. Do not waver, for a person with divided loyalty is as unsettled as a wave of the sea that is blown and tossed by the wind. Such people should not expect to receive anything from the LORD."

God desires that we use the power made available. When we pray, we must have faith, believing that God will do what we ask according to his will. Both his love and power have no limit. His passion motivates him to act on our behalf. David said in Psalm 63:3, "Your unfailing love is better than life itself; how I praise you!"

Though often used interchangeably, there is a subtle difference between faith and belief. Faith is the ability to accept and know in our spirit without the slightest physical, tangible, or visible evidence. Scripture defines authentic faith as the assurance that what we hope for will come about and the certainty that what we cannot see already exists. Belief, in contrast, is an action of the mind and the conscious. To believe means to be wholly or adequately persuaded of a particular opinion. Belief is confidence. Faith in God often encompasses and includes our belief. Faith and belief are so closely connected; they exist in harmony. Rarely can one exist without the other. However, faith, unlike belief, demands action. Faith often moves us to act in a demonstration of what we profess to believe. As encouragement, the apostle Peter said in 1 Peter 1:8-9:

> "There is wonderful joy ahead, even though you must endure many trials for a little while. These trials will show that your faith is genuine. It is being tested as fire tests and purifies gold—though your faith is far more precious than mere gold. So when your faith remains strong through many trials, it will bring you much praise and glory and honor on the day when Jesus Christ is revealed to the whole world. You love him even though you have never seen him. Though you do not see him now, you trust him; and you rejoice with glorious, inexpressible joy. The reward for trusting him will be the salvation of your souls."

God loves, even when we feel unworthy. He does not judge or view us as others might. The Father sees us through perfect, holy, and righteous eyes. He is not critical or biased; we humans are imperfect. When we fall short in morality, kindness, and the way we treat others, God continues to love us. The writer says in Psalm 103:8-10, "The Lord is compassionate and merciful, slow to get angry and filled with unfailing love. He does not punish us for all our sins; he does not deal harshly with us, as we deserve." Instead, he gives generously. He showers us with blessings and treats us better than we do ourselves. He is gracious toward us, giving us what we do not deserve, withholding just punishment.

Because he is a loving father, he will keep nothing good from us. He takes great pleasure in the delight of his children. The writer says in Psalm 37:4, "Seek your happiness in the Lord, and he will give you your heart's desire." (GNT) As we grow in him, our desires increasingly align with his perfect and divine will, making it his joy to answer our petitions. If we ask, believe, and have faith, God will do whatever we ask! We can petition him freely and openly. However, God is not a personal genie, nor will he ever violate his righteous character and holy nature. He will never cooperate or collaborate with a petition to perpetuate sin. He will do all things for us according to His divine word and perfect will. We are told in Hebrews 6:18, "God has given both his promise and his oath. These two things are unchangeable because God can't lie. Therefore, we who have fled to him for refuge can have great confidence as we hold to the hope that lies before us." Jesus said in Mark 11:22, "Have faith in God." Without faith, it is impossible to experience the fullness of all the Father has in store. Jesus assures us in Mark 11:23-25:

> "Truly I tell you, if anyone says to this mountain, Go throw yourself into the sea; and does not doubt in their heart but believes that what they say will happen, it will be done for

them. Therefore, I tell you, whatever you ask for in prayer, believe that you have received it, and it will be yours."

What Is Faith?

Simply stated, true faith is unquestioning confidence in God. According to Hebrews 11:1, "Faith shows the reality of what we hope for; it is the evidence of things we cannot see." When we come to our loving and compassionate father, he desires, we begin with complete and unwavering confidence in his ability and power to do the impossible. He is the sovereign Lord of the universe. He was proving his power by hanging the stars on nothing. If nothing alive exists without origin, then irrefutably, he is the living being from which all living things spring. He is the Ancient of Days, the energy source of the Big Bang, the Eternal and incomprehensible God. The writer said in Psalm 102:25-27:

> "Long ago, you laid the foundation of the earth and made the heavens with your hands. They will perish, but you remain forever; they will wear out like old clothing. You will change them like a garment and discard them. But you are always the same; you will live forever."

Authentic faith is trust in God's word and his promises. Someone said, "Faith is sitting in the middle of the storm of your life and still being able to close your eyes and picture the sunny skies, still being able to feel the better days coming, despite the storm all around you." Because we believe, when we petition our Father in prayer, we wait patiently, knowing that whether he answers now or later, all things are working for our benefit. If he delays his response, we are confident that he will answer. Without tangible evidence, real faith stands with expectation, knowing God can accomplish far beyond expectations, desires, and imagination. Through prayer, we acknowledge God's ability to achieve in our lives what seems impossible but for Him are effortless. The writer says in Hebrews 11:11-12:

> "It was by faith that even Sarah could have a child, though she was barren and was too old. She believed that God would keep his promise. And so an entire nation came from this one man (Abraham) who was as good as dead—a nation with so many people that, like the stars in the sky and the sand on the seashore, there is no way to count them."

God Answers Faith

Prayer is most powerful when joined with faith. There is an old saying, "Much prayer equals much power. Little prayer equals little power." I would dare add the declaration, "Big faith equals big results. Little faith equals limited results." Where there is little faith, there we find a limitation on the power of God in our lives. All things are possible if we only have faith. God is always present and able. We need only have faith and expect the move of his power. Jesus asked in Matthew 9:28-30: "Do you believe I can make you see?" "Yes, Lord," they told him, "we do." Then he touched their eyes and said, "Because of your *faith*, it will happen." Then their eyes were opened, and they could see!"

God is loving and kind. He desires that we be whole and well in every way. However, we must take part in the process. His power is limitless, but we must supply the essential element of faith. Faith alone moves the power of God. Faith is the key to prayer. Jesus said to the blind, "because of your *faith*, it will happen." If you have faith to believe it, you will receive it.

CHAPTER EIGHT
Believers

"TRUST IN THE LORD WITH ALL YOUR HEART; DO NOT DEPEND ON YOUR OWN UNDERSTANDING. SEEK HIS WILL IN ALL YOU DO, AND HE WILL SHOW YOU WHICH PATH TO TAKE. DON'T BE IMPRESSED WITH YOUR OWN WISDOM. INSTEAD, FEAR THE LORD AND TURN AWAY FROM EVIL" (PROVERBS 3:5-7)

PROFESSING BELIEVERS IN the risen Christ have a profound responsibility. That responsibility begins with routinely reminding ourselves and others that pain and suffering are not God's punishment for shortcomings. In life, both good and perceived bad things happen to all people. God is love and shows compassion to the entirety of his creation. Providing an example of God's genuine passion in Matthew 5:43-45, Jesus says:

> "You have heard that it was said, 'Love your neighbor and hate your enemy. But I tell You love your enemies and pray for those who persecute you that you may be children of your Father in heaven. He causes his sun to rise on the evil and the good, and sends rain on the righteous and the unrighteous."

Pain is merely the instrument he uses to deepen our relationship with him. Grief is not God's punishment. During adversity, he reveals his character. Sometimes, he offers us a glimpse into his plans; other times, he develops the love purposed toward us before the world took form.

Acquainted with his love and unmerited kindness, we should honor him and present him rightly to those around us. As believers, we are his ambassadors. It is our responsibility to teach others the truth about our wonderful and gracious God, dispelling lies and untruths about his nature and character. The writer says in Romans 1:5 "Through Christ, God has given us the privilege and authority as apostles to tell Gentiles everywhere what God has done for them, so they will believe and obey him, bringing glory to his name." Even amid challenges, suffering, and pain, we must remain faithful witnesses to the truth. The evidence of his grace towards us and all who call on him is an enduring testimony. Life is full of hurts and sorrows in many forms; however, God is always with us. He will deliver us through it all.

Far too many people profess faith in Christ, yet their lives reflect the contrary. As his children, we must be imitators of his example. Often going off alone to pray, Christ showed the necessity and power of prayer. Through an active commitment to the practice of prayer, the power, presence, and Spirit of God are active and tangible in our lives. No matter the situations or circumstances, the deliberate practice of prayer releases God's limitless power of healing. God's love flows to the places where it hurts the most. The writer said in Psalm 40:1-3:

> "I waited patiently for the LORD; he turned to me and heard my cry. He lifted me out of the slimy pit, out of the mud and mire; he set my feet on a rock and gave me a firm place to stand. He put a new song in my mouth, a hymn of praise

to our GOD. Many will see and fear the LORD and put their trust in him."

As believers, we can know with certainty that God brings comfort to those that seek him. Not only is he faithful, but he is also a savior and a constant friend. We can trust in his power and sovereignty. In Psalm 33:18-21 the writer says,

> "The eyes of the LORD ARE ON THOSE WHO FEAR HIM, ON THOSE WHOSE HOPE IS IN HIS UNFAILING LOVE, to deliver them from death and keep them alive. We wait in hope for the LORD; HE IS OUR HELP AND OUR SHIELD. In him, our hearts rejoice, for we trust in his holy name."

He is faithful, constant, and unchanging. No matter the hurt or pain, God is there amid it with us. When the rain beats down, and the winds of life are raging, not only is our God with us, he is our shield and shelter from the storm. When we find ourselves in the pit, God meets us there.

Like the Psalmist, every believer can experience the depths and heights of God. The Father has no favorites. He shows no partiality, desiring all of his children to know him closely and intimately. Through prayer, we can know him, gain glimpses of his plans, and witness the love he desires to bestow upon us. When pain leads to panic and hurt seems unbearable, our most effective tool is prayer. As children of God, adopted into the family of the great King, we have been elected and chosen to be both salt and light in the dark, fallen, and hurting world.

As the salt of the earth, we influence those around us and within our sphere. As believers in Christ, we aim to show others the matchless, immeasurable, and incomprehensible love of God through the way we live. Our lives should have a significant and profound spiritual impact on others by a consistent demonstration of our authentic and unwavering faith in our God. Lights in the world, we do not hide our lives. We live our lives boldly, openly, and unapologetically for Christ our sovereign redeemer. We are living epistles for the world as a whole to view. As lights, our lives are a transparent and irrefutable demonstration of our understanding and trust in God's infallible word and promises.

CHAPTER NINE
Waiting

"THOSE WHO TRUST IN THE LORD WILL FIND NEW STRENGTH. THEY WILL SOAR HIGH ON WINGS LIKE EAGLES. THEY WILL RUN AND NOT GROW WEARY. THEY WILL WALK AND NOT FAINT" (ISAIAH 40:31).

DURING TRIALS AND times of anguish, pain, and darkness, we desperately need to seek God's presence. In those moments, in desperation, we scream frantically for his help. When he does not come immediately, we become overwhelmed with doubt and disbelief. During these moments, we wonder: Where is God? Is He there? Does He know? Does He even care? The answers to these questions are simple. God is always there! He is the God that never sleeps nor slumbers. His concern is without measure. Sometimes, we just have to wait.

Few people find pleasure in pain. For most of us, waiting on God is overwhelmingly and most difficult when we are heartbroken. However, God is aware of our every hurt, anxiety, and sorrow. It does not take him by surprise. He has ordained these times to encourage us to dialogue with him in prayer, trusting in his sovereignty. Though waiting can frustrate, God promises never to place more on us than we can bear. He knows when to step in and rescue. The Father has proven himself trustworthy. The writer says in Psalm 25:8-10:

> "The LORD is good and does what is right; he shows the proper path to those who go astray. He leads the humble in doing right, teaching them his way. The LORD leads with unfailing love and faithfulness, all who keep his covenant and obey his demands."

God has repeatedly proven his faithfulness. He is the God who never disappoints or fails. Consistently, he keeps his promises, giving a reason for his children to sing and declare his praises. Confident of his power to save, many have bravely shown their faith. Speaking to an angry king as they faced the fierce flames of a raging furnace, the three Hebrew boys Shadrach, Meshach, and Abednego made this declaration in Daniel 3:16 "King Nebuchadnezzar, we need not defend ourselves before you in this matter. If we are thrown into the blazing furnace, the God we serve can deliver us from it, and he will deliver us from Your Majesty's hand." They faced the raging flames, and defiantly declared that God would save them. We also must embrace that same defiance in the face of adversity, knowing that he will deliver us in due time as he did those three young men. Sometimes, we just have to wait.

When we pray, we must be patient. We can trust God to do whatever necessary to produce his intended purpose in our lives. No matter how long the wait, God's plan is working for our good. He is never late, but always on time. God's timing is still perfect, despite our fits of anger, rages, and tantrums. Being the ideal Timekeeper, God moves within his own excellent and divine space. Our emotions do not persuade him. However, he is driven by our faith and willingness to trust him. Our plans can never exceed God's divine plans. The writer records in Isaiah

55:8-9 "My thoughts are nothing like your thoughts," says the Lord. "And my ways are far beyond anything you could imagine. For just as the heavens are higher than the earth, so my ways are higher than your ways, and my thoughts higher than your thoughts."

One essential principle of prayer is consistency. We are encouraged to bring our petitions to God, unwavering in faith. Even if he designates us a time of waiting, we can trust that God will answer. While praying and waiting, God uses these periods to stretch us and help us grow in faith. During these periods, we become more reliant and intimate with him. Periods of waiting also help us grow and mature spiritually. The writer says in Psalm 27:13-14 "I remain confident of this: I will see the goodness of the Lord in the land of the living. Wait for the Lord; be strong and take heart and wait for the Lord." No matter the situation or the period of waiting, God will help us. We can be confident that he will minister to the pain in our hearts, bringing us immeasurable comfort.

Though it can be hard to wait on God while we are in pain, not only will He help us; He will also give us what we need to endure until he rescues. The Psalmist said in Psalm 62:5-7 "Let all that I am wait quietly before God, for my hope is in him. He alone is my rock and my salvation, my fortress where I will not be shaken. My victory and honor come from God alone." Our great God will be the source of strength during our darkest times of sorrow and waiting. He will never leave us comfortless. Though he may not come when we want him, he is always divinely on time. Sometimes, we just have to wait.

CHAPTER TEN
When God Is Silent

"Even though the fig trees have no blossoms, and there are no grapes on the vines; even though the olive crop fails, and the fields lie empty and barren; even though the flocks die in the fields, and the cattle barns are empty, yet I will rejoice in the Lord! I will be joyful in the God of my salvation!" (Habakkuk 3:17-18).

During our darkest moments, we wonder: Where is God? Seemingly, no matter how hard we look, how hard we try, or how frantically we cry, God remains silent. When we need him most, he seems to be nowhere. In moments of our deepest despair, when the pain seems to grip us the strongest and our faith is most shaken, there are times we feel we cannot find him. During those moments, we feel abandoned, forsaken, forgotten. We think God has failed us, leaving us alone to be destroyed by our sorrows. However, we are not alone. In one of his darkest hours, even Israel's great king David questioned in Psalm 13:1-2 "O Lord, how long will you forget me? Forever? How long will you look the other way? How long must I struggle with anguish in my soul, with sorrow in my heart every day?"

When pain and grief are the deepest, and the valley is the darkest, when God is silent, he is there! He will never forsake us nor leave us alone. Though God does not answer when or in the way we want, it does not mean we are unheard. His silence does not mean he is unconcerned. The Father is always concerned. He declares to us in Isaiah 41:10 "Don't be afraid, for I am with you. Don't be discouraged, for I am your God. I will strengthen you and help you. I will hold you up with my victorious right hand." There is no moment or situation that God is not near to us. There is no place that we can find ourselves that he is not present with us. He is our faithful friend that stands with us closer than a brother.

God's silence is not abandonment. On the contrary, his silence is the time he uses to orchestrate a divine plan on our behalf or perform some marvelous work incognito. Nature testifies to the fact that God does some of his best work in silence. For example, we reference the butterfly. First, we see the caterpillar. Then, at the perfect time, he goes into his cocoon. Inside the silence of the envelope, God does the incomprehensible. He transforms the caterpillar into a beautiful butterfly, creating a uniquely patterned creature having no equal or duplicate. When God is silent, he is creating something original, unique, and beautiful. Like the butterfly that emerges, having no duplicate or equal, specific, and unique are the plans God makes for each of our lives. He does terrific and matchless work, particular to each of our lives, situations, and circumstances.

When we perceive God silent, it does not mean he is not speaking. Often, he is speaking; we just cannot hear him because we are expecting him in the wrong way. God does not always respond in the way we hope, nor does he always react in the same way. The prophet Elijah gives us an example of how we often miss God, particularly amid our desperation. Often in our panic, frustration, fear, sadness, and pain, we cannot hear or perceive God as we should. The Bible tells us of Elijah's encounter with God, in 1Kings 19:11-13:

> "Go out and stand before me on the mountain," the Lord told him. And as Elijah stood there, the Lord passed by, and a mighty windstorm hit the mountain. It was such a terrible blast that the rocks were torn loose, but the Lord was not in the wind. After the wind, there was an earthquake, but the Lord was not in the earthquake. And after the earthquake, there was a fire, but the Lord was not in the fire. And after the fire, there was the sound of a gentle whisper. When Elijah heard it, he wrapped his face in his cloak and went out and stood at the entrance of the cave. And a voice said, "What are you doing here, Elijah?"

God does not always present himself in a way that we are familiar, nor does he speak necessarily in a way that we expect. Elijah thought God was in the windstorm, earthquake, and fire. However, none of those were God. God spoke, not in thunder or lightning. He spoke in the smallest of whispers. He asked Elijah out of concern, "What has brought you here?" God may not answer in the way we expect. However, we can rest knowing he will answer; because of how much he cares. When God is silent, he is working and creating an opportunity for us to experience him more profoundly and awesomely. God's silence provides us a chance and opportunity to dialogue and fellowship with him more frequently and personally in prayer. Sometimes, God uses silence to lovingly motivate us to speak to him, sharing the depth and fullness of our hearts. No matter the circumstance, even when he is silent, God is there. Pain, sadness, and fear are a part of this temporal existence. However, there is an eternal God, constant, and never-changing. Amidst pain and sorrow, the writer says in

Psalm 46:1-2 "God is our refuge and strength, always ready to help in times of trouble. So we will not fear when earthquakes come and the mountains crumble into the sea."

God is never silent. Even when we cannot hear him or see him, he is at work even during the darkest and most painful circumstances. God never sleeps nor slumbers. The writer says in Proverbs 15:3 "The Lord is watching everywhere, keeping his eye on both the evil and the good." God is omniscient. The Father knows precisely when and how to save. Being the divine and perfect Timekeeper, he is always on time. No matter the scenario, God's silence or the perception of his silence does not equate to inaction. He knows the depths and magnitude of our pains and sorrows and has the perfect cure. He will not leave us alone in the pit of despair, heartache, and sadness. He will help us. The Psalmist boldly penned in Psalm 121:1-5:

> "I look up to the mountains—does my help come from there? My help comes from the Lord, who made heaven and earth! He will not let you stumble; the one who watches over you will not slumber. Indeed, he who watches over Israel never slumbers or sleeps. The Lord himself watches over you!"

CHAPTER ELEVEN
God Can Be Trusted

"THOSE WHO KNOW YOUR NAME PUT THEIR TRUST IN YOU, FOR YOU, O LORD, HAVE NOT FORSAKEN THOSE WHO SEEK YOU" (PSALM 9:10).

NO MATTER HOW seemingly unbearable our pain, grief, or sorrow, we can trust God to help. As a loving and compassionate father, he is kind to all. If we only have faith, he will resolve even our most significant challenges; if we allow him. Without exception, God wants to be our source of strength, the hope for our today, and the acknowledged comfort of our tomorrows. He desperately wants to be invited to our lives. No matter the circumstance, he wants our faith that nothing is impossible for those that believe. The writer says in Psalm 9:9-10 "The LORD is a refuge for the oppressed, a stronghold in times of trouble. Those who know your name trust in you, for you, Lord, have never forsaken those who seek you."

God never fails because he is infallible. His love is incomparable. Reflecting honestly, we should acknowledge that God has been tremendously gracious and kind. He has given all far more than deserved. He owes nothing, yet he blesses in ways often taken for granted. Rarely do we thank him for the beauty of the trees, the warmth of summer, the frost of winter, shelter, food, health, functioning limbs, blood in our veins, or breath in our lungs. Yet the writer says in Psalm 24:1-2 "The earth is the Lord's, and everything in it. The world and its entire people belong to him."

Without exception, God has done more for us than we could ever do for ourselves, caring for us until this very hour. We have not done it ourselves. None but God can prolong our lives a moment beyond the appointed hour of transition. Only God has the power to create life or infuse a rose with the vibrant radiance of its redness. Sorrow and heartache have a way of clouding and distorting our memories. Quickly we forget his kindness. However, that does not change or negate his commitment to helping us in our times of need. No matter the bigness, smallness, pain, or depth of darkness, we can bring everything to God in prayer. He will answer, even if he delays. Waiting is not necessarily a denial of any request or petition. Waiting with faith and patience is merely accepting his choice of the moment to show up.

There is nothing too hard or too big for God. In his weakness, he is more reliable than any man. In fallacy, he astounds the wisest of all humanity. He alone is God. He comes to the rescue of all who call on him. The writer said in Psalm 18:6 "In my distress, I cried out to the Lord; Yes, I prayed to my God for help. He heard me from his sanctuary; my cries to him reach his ears." David said in Psalm 34:4-6 "I prayed to the Lord, and he answered me. He freed me from all my fears. Those who look to him for help will be radiant with joy; no shadow of shame will darken their faces. In my desperation, I prayed, and the Lord listened; he saved me from all my troubles." David's declaration and experience with God is a testimony to the fact that God can be trusted. He comes to the aid of his children. Whoever calls on God will find help. The eye of the Lord is everywhere. He sees our conditions and circumstances. Even in our darkest hours, if we trust him, have faith, and call to him through prayer, he will answer.

We are never alone in our struggles, even when we feel abandoned. Perplexed, even David questioned his situation, saying in Psalm 13:1-3 "How long, LORD? Will you forget me forever? How long will you hide your face from me? How long must I wrestle with my thoughts and day after day have sorrow in my heart? Look on me and answer, LORD my God. Give light to my eyes, or I will sleep in death." In his distress, David wanted to know: Where is God? Why is God silent? Why has God not come? However, reflecting, David had to conclude that God had consistently proven reliable. Encouraged, he declared in Psalm 27:1-2 "The LORD is my light and my salvation — so why should I be afraid? The LORD is my fortress, protecting me from danger, so why should I tremble? When evil people come to devour me, when my enemies and foes attack me, they will stumble and fall."

We can trust God. In him, our hope and faith are well-founded. He is a solid rock and mighty fortress. Through prayer, we will find safety and comfort. No matter when we call, he is willing and able to help us. He lifts the bowed down head. He mends the wounds of the brokenhearted. Whatever the need, God will provide. Wherever the place, he will meet us. God never misses an appointed date. Those who call on him, he is available to comfort. The writer says in Psalm 145:13-20:

> "The LORD always keeps his promises; he is gracious in all he does. The LORD helps the fallen and lifts those bent beneath their loads. The eyes of all look to you in hope; you give them their food as they need it. When you open your hand, you satisfy the hunger and thirst of every living thing. The LORD is righteous in everything he does; he is filled with kindness. The LORD is close to all who call on him, yes, to all who call on him in truth. He grants the desires of those who fear him; he hears their cries for help and rescues them."

CHAPTER TWELVE
God Is Concerned

"THE LORD, YOUR GOD, IS LIVING AMONG YOU. HE IS A MIGHTY SAVIOR. HE WILL TAKE DELIGHT IN YOU WITH GLADNESS. WITH HIS LOVE, HE WILL CALM ALL YOUR FEARS" (ZEPHANIAH 3:17).

No matter where we find ourselves, God cares. When the hurt and pains and sorrow lead us to believe we cannot go on, we have the faithful promises of God. When life has crushed us and the darkness of pain is consuming, we are reminded in Psalm 30:5 "Weeping may last through the night, but joy comes with the morning." God is concerned. God does care. He will never leave us in sorrow, misery, or despair. Our Father will never allow our destruction. The character and nature of God is love. Speaking of his immeasurable love, we are reminded in Romans 5:8 "God showed his great love for us by sending Christ to die for us while we were still sinners." When we are not mindful of God or is presence, or when we reject him, and walk away from him, we are always on his mind. In Luke 12:6-7 Jesus says:

"What is the price of five sparrows—two copper coins? Yet God does not forget a single one of them. And the very hairs on your head are all numbered. So don't be afraid; you are more valuable to God than a whole flock of sparrows."

God is with us in the bottomless pit and during the darkest night of despair. He may not come at the time that we want him, yet he will come to our rescue. David said in Psalm 118:5 "In my distress, I prayed to the Lord, and the Lord answered me and set me free." God is our helper. He is a redeemer, and the deliverer from all of life's problems, hurts, and sorrows. Though pain and suffering are a part of the human experience, God does not leave us alone to face the harshness, terror, and sadness in isolation. The writer says in Psalm34:19 "The righteous person suffers many troubles, but the Lord comes to the rescue each time."

It is wrong to believe that God causes suffering. His compassionate nature testifies against that belief and idea. Speaking about the character of God, David says in Psalm 86:15 "You, O Lord, are a God full of compassion and grace, long-suffering and abundant in mercy and truth." God is never the source of pain. However, when he permits and allows us to experience pain, he does not condemn us to endure it alone. Having a divine plan and purpose, he will deliver in due time. He is the great and matchless burden bearer. The writer says in 1 Corinthians 10:13 "The temptations in your life do not differ from what others experience. And God is faithful. He will not allow the temptation to be more than you can stand. When you are tempted, he will show you a way out so you can endure."

Pain and suffering is not punishment from an angry God. The writer says in Micah 7:18-19 "Where is another God like you, who pardons the guilt of the remnant, overlooking the sins of his special people? You will not stay angry with your people forever, because you delight in showing unfailing love." If God were angry with those he loves, he would never seek to destroy them. He makes every attempt to reconcile wooing them with the power and beauty of his love. Even in the seemingly hopeless scenario, God has promised in Jeremiah 29:11 "I know the plans I have for you," says the Lord. "They are plans for good and not for disaster, to give you a future and a hope."

Despite what many believe and have been taught about God, too often, his character is inaccurately portrayed. When things go wrong, and the season of pain comes, we quickly assume God is angry and punishing for some sin or offense. This presumption could be no further from the truth. God does not penalize in such ways. He loves us. He does not treat us as we so many times have deserved. Irrefutably, God repeatedly extends mercy and grace. Beginning in verse 7 of Psalm 103, the Psalmist says:

> "He revealed his character to Moses and his deeds to the people of Israel. The Lord is compassionate and merciful, slow to get angry, and filled with unfailing love. He does not punish us for all our sins; he does not deal harshly with us, as we deserve. For his unfailing love toward those who fear him is as great as the height of the heavens above the earth. He has removed our sins as far from us as the east is from the west. The Lord is like a father to his children, tender and compassionate to those who fear him. For he knows how weak we are; he remembers we are only dust" (Psalm 103:7-14).

When the hard and challenging times come, men and women readily question the love and compassion of God. Far too often, the questions are: "What kind of God would allow this?" "What kind of God would do that?" "Where was God when this happened?" "Where was God when that happened?" The answer to these questions is simple. He was there! Not a single thing escapes him. The writer said in Psalm 139:7-12:

"I can never escape from your Spirit! I can never get away from your presence! If I go up to heaven, you are there. If I go down to the grave, you are there. If I ride the wings of the morning, if I dwell by the farthest oceans, even there your hand will guide me and your strength will support me. I could ask the darkness to hide me and the light around me to become night— but even in darkness, I cannot hide from you. To you, the night shines as bright as day. Darkness and light are the same to you."

To the critic, a reasonable question in response could be, "What kind of God would show such grace, mercy, and compassion to all that deserves his wrath and judgment?" God never judges men and women, as is his right. Continuously he extends his love. The manifestation or presence of pain does not negate the love and compassion of God. Because of his loving character and nature, when rejected, he still responds in kindness. When punishment is warranted, God shows mercy. He withholds punishment. It is never God's desire to punish, destroy, or cause pain. When we falsely accuse God of such a heinous act, we lie against his nature.

Speaking about God's nature, the apostle Peter says in 2 Peter 3:9 "The Lord isn't slow about his promise, as some people think. No, he is patient for your sake. He does not want anyone to be destroyed, but wants everyone to repent." There is nothing we can do to make God love us any more than he does. None of us can earn brownie points with God. It is ridiculous to believe that being a so-called good person or doing philanthropic deeds can insulate us from pain. Nothing could be further from the truth. We will all experience our share of pain, hurt and sorrow. But God cares for us, and we are never alone. He has promised to always be with us, deliver, and rescue us. He never violates his promises or fails to honor and keep his word. We can trust God!

Final Thoughts

AT VARIOUS STAGES, life can challenge and be painful. However, during those times, we can turn to God for an answer to every problem. He is a matchless problem solver. He alone holds the solution to even the most troubling issue. He is the lifter of the lowest bowed head. God can handle every trial that we experience. He is also willing and available. The Father is always there. He only asks us to trust in him and pray, believing by faith that he is our loving God and father. Anxiously God waits for the call of his children. No matter how dark the day might be, our God is always there, ever ready to bless us.

The Lord has promised that he is faithful to those that hope in him. His love exceeds the imagination of those that believe in him. His thoughts are consistent and always aligned for our most celebrated and highest benefit. Because of his immeasurable love, God orchestrates our lives to bring us into a perfect relationship with him. Nothing that he allows us to experience is to harm us. Whatever he will enable it to strengthen us and to lead us to a higher and more in-depth knowledge of his power and plans for our lives.

God is the wellspring and source of our greatest and most fulfilled lives. In him rests the power of our happiness, peace, and joy. With God, all things are possible. Whatever we desire, if it aligns with his divine and righteous will, we can have it. All we have to do is ask in prayer. Nothing good will he ever withhold from his children. Pain is not the worst thing. God is aware of our suffering. No matter the time or stage that sorrow presents in our lives, God is there to carry us through it. He is always with us. Because of his love, God never neglects or abandons us like orphans. On the contrary, he stands with us and holds us. We have a shield even when we believe that we have done it ourselves. He never leaves us alone. He is our rock and anchor. He is the shelter from the strongest storm, our hiding place, and unfailing comfort whenever we need him most. We can always run to Him.

When we perceive him silent, God is working in the shadows. Because of his unconditional love, he is graciously willing to be everything we will allow him to be and more. No matter where we are or how low we have fallen, God is there. There is no pain, heartache, or sorrow that God cannot heal. Our faith moves God. No matter the tragedy or sadness, when we pray, he answers. We can always trust God. Sometimes, we just have to wait.

Made in the USA
Coppell, TX
22 December 2020